DRAGONS&DAISIES

Keys to Resolve Baffling Behavior
In Early Childhood Education

Letha Marchetti, OTR/L

Rafael
Books

an imprint of Occupational Therapy Home Services

This book is dedicated to those who give themselves to making a positive difference in the lives of children. This may mean you!

Special thanks to early childhood mental health professionals at Jewish Family and Children's Services in San Rafael, California for helping me clarify this work and bring it to the public in a larger way. (In alphabetical order):

Dr. Daniella De Vasques	who grasped what I had to say and opened a world of collaboration for healthier children and more informed teachers.
Bonne Goltz Reiser	whose vision and collaborative expertise continues to bring this information into preschools in Marin County. Bonne's ability to see beyond words to their consequences is effectual and splendid. This extraordinary ability benefits me and countless children.
Sandra Ramirez-Griggs	whose heart for children brings support to them, their teachers, their parents and anyone caring enough to take her expertise to heart.
Jennifer Reynolds	who can twinkle at a child and encourage him to his soul.
Bonnie Romanow	whose work with children, teachers and their families is masterfully effective.
Elisa Sapienza	whose love for children translates into a smile that takes over every feature of her face.

Two women who give and give, selflessly:

Marisol Avash	who voluntarily translated some of my material into Spanish so teachers would not be left out, who has spent hours going over material with me before trainings to benefit spanish-speaking teachers, and who has continually encouraged me to get this information into the public realm to help our children.
Dorothy Foytik	whose motto is "I just did what needed doing." From piroshki to pavlova, from Davis to Dillon beach; Aunt Dorothy, your energetic ways and generous heart have been an encouragement to me and so many others. Your work making a place for children - creating toys, hosting playgroups, establishing nursery schools at home and abroad is still fruitful. With this book, I hope to add another layer of understanding to the work you started and continue doing what needs to be done.

Illustrations © 2015 Warren Dayton • Design: Martha Dayton | ArtiFactInk.com

ISBN # 978-0-9965351-0-6

USA Library of Congress Control Number: 2015944889

Priting: First Edition - July, 2015

Ordering Information: LethaMarchetti.com

Table of Contents

Dragons and Daisies *is a gift for early childhood educators and parents. In this charming and enlightening book, Letha Marchetti illuminates the neurodevelopment of young children. These important building blocks of early development aren't always covered in early education texts.*

With clear and colorful explanations, fascinating stories and creative solutions, Letha helps us comprehend and support children whose behaviors are perplexing, challenging, and best understood in the context of their sensory experience.

Lyda Beardsley, Ph.D.

Director, Early Childhood Education and Child Development Program

College of Marin

From Baffling To Blooming

I was called into a preschool to observe two children in a class of eighteen. A boy in an orange, striped shirt was not able to join in with the others. He flapped his arms when he got up from the lunch table. As the children went to a group circle, he ran frenzied circuits punctuated with sudden jerks as if startled by the presence of his fellow children. Going to a cozy pillow bed, he snuggled down and pulled a blanket over himself, completely. He acted like a shy little dragon, peeking out briefly then hiding again.

The other child I was called in to observe was quiet. As she held a pencil, the tip didn't reach the paper because her little fist was palm up with the pencil nestled under four curled fingers well above the paper. She moved her hand along, without making a mark, distressed that she wasn't pleasing her teacher and seemingly not knowing why.

Two other children in the room caught my eye because they also were challenged by what they saw, heard and felt.

Two years later I was called back to the same classroom of about eighteen children. Of course, these are a different batch of children. This time, of the eighteen children; instead of four catching my attention, there were only four that didn't appear to need occupational therapy.

It's likely that this school has more children with baffling behavior because of their success in the last couple years. Still, every preschool with which I consult notes an increase in children with developmental challenges. In fact, in the past 2 years, I've noticed more than a one hundred percent increase in issues related to self-control at the schools where I consult.

Children who are angry, frustrated, unable to sit still, easily overwhelmed, clumsy, and uncoordinated; children with alarmingly short fuses; and children who cannot stay with an activity for more than a few seconds at a time; these are just some examples of what early childhood teachers currently face every day.

Parents hope teachers will fix these behaviors. Teachers, in turn, hope parents will resolve the issues and, pretty soon, everyone's frustration level has ratcheted up. Compounding the issue is the fact that preschools are expected to send their graduates off to kindergarten "ready to go" and able to "self regulate". The strain is enough to take the joy out of an otherwise fabulous job.

The good news is: there's help. A basic understanding of how children develop reveals ways in which we can support them through tough times so they can bloom. As an early childhood educator you are perfectly poised to make a difference in your students lives. The changes you will be able to make, based on the things you'll learn in this book, will likely benefit your entire class and will help you to shepherd children towards greater success.

Aiden's Story

Hi, I'm Aiden, and this is my friend D. Dragon. Life has never been sooo good!

When I was little, I used to be anxious when I heard loud noises. They scared me. In fact, I was scared a lot of the time. At school there were so many people I didn't know. Everyone else seemed to know what to do: when to get in line, what table to go to... I didn't. Sometimes when I got to school, I'd stop at the door. I just couldn't move.

A lot of the time I'd end up in tears, kicking the floor and wanting everything to stop. I didn't feel good.

I used to get in trouble at school - it seemed like all the time. Teacher told me to sit still, sit down, and keep my feet to myself. I really couldn't do it and I didn't understand what I did wrong. Mom said I acted like D. Dragon.

Something good happened, though. My teacher found out how to help me. She learned from The Baffling Behavior Expert that the things I like to do most are actually good for me. I get to jump and swing. Now it's OK if I stand at the table instead of sit and it's OK if I fidget with my toes. Teacher said she learned that my senses can get me upset or help me calm. I get to spend more time outside now too. I really like that!

I'm not the way I used to be, so scared and upset. I like school I can say the whole alphabet and spell my name.

My friend D. Dragon and I have learned the secret of the daisy and we're excited to share it with you.

Curiosity!

"She just copies her older sister!" Dad explained. "Aurora won't eat vegetables so neither will Amy. Aurora wants to wear a hat inside and now Amy does too."

"We had his older brother in class too," the teacher told me. "He was the same way - getting epic upset over nothing. Any little thing set him off. It's got to be genetic!"

Here's the challenge; when we make up our minds about what's causing something, it's difficult, or even impossible, to grasp a new concept. Yes, children do copy and yes, there is genetic influence. But there are also many other factors at work. Just as a cough can be the result of a cold, swallowing wrong, a supercilious gnat, or something else, behavior can have multiple origins.

To be successful with this ground-breaking information, I'm suggesting we choose to be curious. I wonder if Amy feels better with her hat on?

This is your first key to resolving baffling behaviors:

To see behavior in its relationship to the nervous system and development, consciously leave preconceptions behind.

"Regulation" - An Ugly Word For A Beautiful Concept

What teacher wants to hear that his or her children need regulation? It sounds oppressive, bringing to mind a list of requirements. Yet in its simplest form, regulation is having self-control. The beautiful thing about regulation, or being in control, is that it's the neurological state in which we are able to learn. I call it the learning zone. Children are miserable when they are out of control. They much prefer learning and its associated sense of accomplishment.

Self-Control = The Learning Zone

WHAT I DO

Keeping my hands & feet under my control
Not talking out of turn or too loudly

MY BODY

Controlling bathroom functions
Tolerating small discomforts

MY THOUGHTS

Maintaining focus, staying with the topic
Not intrusive or obsessive

MY FEELINGS

I control my emotions
My emotions don't control me

Children bounced into the room like cereal poured out of a box. The movement helped with the transition. Their next step, as had been the routine for the past month, was to sit on one of the letters encircling the rug while the teacher read a story.

Teacher Sandra noticed Aiden was not quite with the group. She asked, "Can you come find the green 'S?'" As if he had no clue what Sandra had just said, Aiden jumped, toward the circle. He gradually reached the yellow "G" on the rug. Sandra went to the "S," gently, slowly, guiding Aiden. Noticing that he was jumping, Sandra had the whole class stand up and jump on his or her letter. Aiden jumped off his letter.

Spontaneously, Sandra began to sing a simple rhythm to bring the group into the learning zone.

> *"I... have found... my place.*
> *I... have found... my place.*
> *We... are in a.. cir-cle.*
> *We... are in a.. cir-cle.*
> *I... have found... my place.*
> *We... are in a.. circle."*

By the second round of the song, Aiden was fidgeting, looking around, and not yet joining in. Teacher Sandra began to clap her hands in a slow rhythm to her made-up chorus. Aiden clapped a few times. He missed several beats and almost got his last clap on the beat. His body began to sway, very slightly. Standing, looking at Sandra, Aiden didn't fidget. He sat down as the other children did when the song ended.

Now reading time could begin.

Getting into the learning zone doesn't just happen. Children need support to develop self-control. When children's behavior is baffling, the question often arises; "Will they outgrow this?" The answer is; "They need help." So let's see what we can do to help children reach their potential and become everything they were created to be.

There is a neurological zone for learning
This is where children want to be.

Sandra is masterful at guiding children into the learning zone. She knew Aiden was overwhelmed trying to process the move from one room to another. She also knew that his classmate's noise combined with her directions to the letter "S" were only adding to his difficulties.

So, she supported him with a rhythm. His nervous system was able to pick up on the regular beat and follow it.

Slowing everything down also helped this child. Aiden takes longer to process all that comes at him. Giving him time helps keep him in the learning zone.

3, 2, 1...
Blast off!

Activation occurs when there is more activity in the nervous system. This is normal and good. With activation, we are prepared for action, for learning, and for thinking. A mature nervous system activates and deactivates in cycle after cycle.

Chloe arrived at her classroom and teacher Maria led her by the hand to the net bag so she could see a butterfly hatching.

As she watched the butterfly crawl out of its chrysalis, her face found its smile. Her little body began to wriggle as she oooed and giggled. Chloe told her friend Amanda; "The budderfy is hatched!"

"We can fly to Monterey," Miss Maria told the class as she led them out the back door. Miss Maria held up a long coiled spiral. "This is what a butterfly's tongue is like. The butterfly unrolls its tongue and drinks nectar from deep inside flowers."

Next the children blew party horns with brightly colored paper tubes that unrolled and rolled back up just like a butterfly's proboscis. Some of them giggled. Chloe blew her party favor again and again. She even blew her "butterfly tongue" into a big red cup filled with tissue paper petals; just like a butterfly does to get nectar from a flower.

Chloe's activation was typical; she was engaged and ready for whatever came next. Activation has a range that is useful. This self-controlled range of activation is the learning zone.

*Jory wakes up and burrows deeper into his bed. "Unnooo,"
he groans when Dad says it's time to get up. Eventually,
he meanders to the bathroom. As he brushes his teeth, the
cinnamon toothpaste has a little zing to it and he feels more
alive. Walking to the kitchen he chooses a crunchy cereal and
begins to think about school. In the car, on the way to school,
there is little conversation. Jory doesn't run around the play
yard with the other children. He sits and talks with Miss Lizzy.*

Jory has a different rhythm. He tends to live below the zone of
learning. The cinnamon toothpaste and crunchy cereal temporar-
ily brought his arousal level up a couple of ticks. Similarly, he is
able to enter into a functional range of activation with support.
Talking with his teacher is one such support.

*Jory's sister, Kayla, is awake and out of bed before Dad enters
the room. Her clothes are in a few piles. She tries on different
outfits and keeps adding more to the piles.*

*After her turn with the cinnamon toothpaste she starts getting
a little anxious; "Dad, did you get the fruit roll-ups? Where is
my school bag? Daaaad! I can't find my bruuush!" When they
arrive at school, Kayla sees her friend and runs across the play
yard forgetting to put her stuff in her cubby.*

*When the children come into class, Kayla's backpack is sitting
by the play structure. Kayla looks confused for a moment when
Miss Lizzy asks her, "Where is your pack?"*

Kayla was over activated. She was out of her learning zone. The
zinging toothpaste took her up a notch. The stress of not finding
her brush also added to her activation. Kayla's behavior shows
the results of her high activation.

When behavior is baffling, it helps to know that there are two
factors at play. One is sensation. Sensation can drive behavior
without any connection to the reasoning part of the brain. The
other is activation. Once a child is over-activated, there is no
connection to rational thinking.

When I teach seminars and conventions, I see eyes light up and fresh smiles as teachers realize that much of developmental behavior has no relationship to the thinking process. It's truly based in sensory needs. No wonder behavior can be so baffling!

 **Behavior, especially in young children, is often sensory driven.**

What Goes Up
Must Come Down

Deactivation is when activity in the nervous system lessens and we calm. When Jory and Kyla come back into the room, neither is ready to learn. Jory needs to come *up* into his learning zone. Kyla is beyond her zone of learning; she needs to come *down*.

It is physiologically impossible for children to learn when they are not in the learning zone.

When children are upset, crying beyond control,

or so angry they have lost it; it is NOT helpful to:

- tell them where they made a mistake
- force an apology
- try to teach them anything

While observing at a preschool, I noticed two boys who wanted the same basketball. The scuffle ended up with Danny on the ground. By the time the aide brought them to the teacher near me, one was in tears and the other was so angry he flushed red.

Danny muttered a few words in response to the teacher's query; "He... ball... I... took ball... don't know." Gary spoke forcefully; "I want it! He came right in my way. It's not fair!"

Danny had trouble speaking, not because he had a speech problem, but because his nervous system was so activated his voice almost went away. If you have ever been put on the spot to give a verbal reply and found you just couldn't speak, then you have experienced a version of what happened to Danny.

The teacher required the boys to apologize to each other, gave them some words of wisdom, and sent them on their way. What the teacher didn't know was that the activation level of both children was so high that they could not learn. They needed to deactivate before any of her good words could be useful. When activation is high enough to be beyond the zone of learning, the reasoning area of the brain is offline.

Here is an example of a teacher helping children to enter the learning zone.

> *Miss Maria starts music that sounds like a ballet. She leads the children in lifting their arms up high over their heads with palms together. "We are flowers opening up for butterflies!" As they move in rhythm with the music, each child finds his or her version of a flower. Miss Maria adds breathing exercises to help bring the room into regulation. As she opens her arms she demonstrates by breathing in and saying, "Hmm." Bringing her arms close to her body, she blows out a "Wwwoo." "*

Breathing in brings activation within our body. Breathing out brings deactivation. As you can see, there is a normal flow of activation and deactivation within our system. It is as if our internal energy level cycles up and down like the path around petals on a daisy. Moving toward the tip of a petal we activate: something is building inside the body. Coming back toward the center of the flower we deactivate: the body is calming. We trace this pattern up and down, round and round throughout the day.

I invite you to trace your finger around the petals of the daisy photo on the next page. Allow your finger to move toward the tip of the petal quickly. But, when you return toward the center, try going in super slow motion.

What happens inside you as you do this? Do you feel a change? Did you notice a deeper breath? It may make you just want to

Photo: Jenny Wyman Rush - who captured this beautiful simplicity

rest and stop tracing along the petals. That's ok. That deeper breath is a signal that you are in the learning zone. If so, this is good because you will more fully grasp the concepts I'm presenting.

When the nervous system activates and deactivates, going up and down, cycle after cycle - like tracing daisy petals - the nervous system is in the learning zone. In other words, we are in a state of self-control.

Staying on the daisy petals means we are able to learn.

The challenge is that children's nervous systems don't trace around and around, like following the edges of daisy petals. A little child has not developed neurologically enough to stay on the daisy petals. We are familiar with this in infants. We soothe babies to help them calm. Young children are often in the same situation. Simply because their systems are immature, they are likely to activate up to the tip of a petal and then fall right off the flower and out of the learning zone.

So, here's what we do...

Can I Borrow
A Cup Of Stability?

Children are not born with self-control. Their nervous systems are still growing. It is not possible for young children to stabilize without help. The good news is that they can borrow from you. You are a grounding force in your classroom. Children subconsciously sense your stability and it helps them to calm.

Have you ever walked into a quiet room and felt the tension? This is your subconscious awareness of what is going on. From conception, a baby begins subconscious communication, often referred to as pinging, with Mom. We can think of a baby as a little submarine, sending out a ping to be sure she's safe. Mom also pings back subconsciously to her child. In a perfect world, Mom is thrilled to be pregnant. She thinks of how she has wanted this baby and how she already loves the growing wonder inside her. In this way, the baby gets a solid "everything is good" sort of ping back from Mom. This starts to set up stability within the baby. Since the infant's nervous system will be developing for years to come, this is a good start.

Inevitably, the world is not perfect and Mom will, at some point, get upset about something. This can happen at any time during gestation, labor or delivery, and beyond. When it does, as mom calms, the baby senses her stability, and calms also. This is how we start learning to stay on the daisy petals.

Sometimes, after delivery Mom and infant must be separated. During this time, the baby ping, ping, pings but doesn't receive back the ping she's known all her life. When Mom and baby are reunited, Mom cuddles her child and communicates how difficult it was being apart. Phew! the baby senses things are back on track. As baby and mom stay together, the pinging continues and Mom's stability helps her daughter. The baby's nervous system begins to deactivate and stabilize. The intensity of the separation is repaired through this process. The baby's little nervous system is developing a new pattern of being able to settle after a big upset. She's already gaining the sort of strength she'll need to cope with life's challenges successfully.

It's bath time and Stacy is cradled on the sponge in her perfect baby tub. Mom reaches for the shampoo and knocks it to the floor with a big splat! Stacy startles, her arms and legs shoot out and her eyes go wide looking at Mom. Mom has knocked over plenty of things before now, so she isn't upset. She's so pleased to be bathing Stacy and loves seeing her baby enjoying the warm water and giggling. She looks lovingly at her daughter and says, "Oh, Momma dropped the shampoo. That's OK. We'll skip it this time." Stacy perceives Mom's stable system and it is almost as if Stacy feels: "If it's OK with you, then it's OK with me."

Stacy's system can't yet calm itself but she just borrowed some of Mom's stability. This simple incident created a wave of activation, then deactivation in her young system. Stacy was helped onto the daisy petals by Mom staying on the petals herself. This helped Stacy's nervous system make some new synaptic connections which she can retrace as she develops. She's learning how to activate and deactivate while staying in the learning zone.

As an early childhood educator, you are the consistent, stable caregiver off of whom children will ping. Your warm acceptance and your ability to stay on the daisy petals yourself will have lifelong positive effects on the children you care for.

As I've already mentioned, children subconsciously sense your stability and it helps them to calm. You are the force of calm in your classroom. Some of your children may have issues at home.

There may be separated parents, ill parents, or mentally unstable parents and you may be the most stable influence they know.

Children's still-developing nervous systems send out a signal as if to say, "Is everything OK?" If you are dealing with a room of very activated children who have fallen off their daisy petals, your system is going to be upset. This will ping back to the children and their behavior may shift towards that of a fiery, scaly beast or a timid, shy dragon. Either way, they are out of the learning zone.

> ## If you are going through a personally upsetting time, take the opportunity to get yourself calm. Here are a few tips (and you'll find more as you read through):

1. Get extra sleep. Eight hours is a good start. Your body wants to settle onto the daisy petals as you sleep. Give it what it needs to do that. In cold climates, putting a heating pad under the small of the back can be helpful. Getting to bed earlier so you can get more hours of sleep before midnight has also proven helpful.

2. Take some time to feel the rhythm of music. This is not working with music in the background but rather a more immersive experience. Play an instrument, sing, dance, rock, clap along, or sit back, close your eyes and simply enjoy it. Taking in the rhythm is the key. Rhythm helps bring the nervous system into the learning zone.

3. Take a bath in water that is warmer than your body temperature. Spend at least 10 minutes in a semi-reclined position. This encourages your kidneys to shift off the adrenal glands, creating physical space, and changing the release of cortisol (a hormone related to stress). In short, it calms the body.

Lending children your stability is subconscious. Perhaps you have noticed when something goes wrong in your life, the children you work with become fussy and unsettled. When you are off the daisy petals, children pick up on it and can be irritable, fussy, unsettled, and unfocused. This grows like a tornado. When the teacher is off the petals, the children, unable to stabilize on their own, "catch" the upset and tend to spin out of control. As children in the classroom act up, the teacher tends to get more activated. Thus the children get less stable and the vortex grows. Of course, parents deal with their own tornados at home. Your empathy and personal success as a teacher supports children in class. It also carries over to parents who come to you with their questions and frustrations about their children's behavior when they are not at school.

So, how can you help the children you work with and even yourself and your colleagues to feel more settled and calm? First, add physical movement. Start by putting a smile on your face and taking a moment to breathe deeply. Your brain will interpret the smile as happiness and improve your neurological status. A little music and some dancing can bring the group toward the daisy petals.

Another option is parachute play:

- Each child holds the open parachute with both hands.
- Everyone moves to the right three steps (spinning the chute).
- Everyone moves to the left three steps.
- Everyone holds the parachute with the left hand and turns to the right, walking in a circle so the chute spins.
- Everyone holds the parachute with the right hand turns to the left, walking in a circle so the chute spins.
- Call out names of children on opposite sides who run under the parachute while the group lifts it.
- Put a beach ball on the parachute and everyone makes it bounce and catches it again in the parachute.

Just as you take care of your students, you need to take care of yourself. If you have an enormous loss in your life, you truly don't want your classroom going through it too. Things will go wrong in a big way. At such times, self-care is crucial. It is also equally important to not let minor things destroy your stability. The driver who cut you off on the way to work, or your washing machine breaking down… these are the types of things you can learn to breathe through. Here's how.

Use this exercise to help calm your nervous system:

1. Stand up if possible. This gives your nervous system more calming input through your joints, tendons and muscles.

2. Place your feet a little wider than your hips.

3. Rock your weight slowly from side to side, feeling it fully on one foot, then the other.

4. Notice if you took a deeper breath. If so, stop and feel that internally. [Stopping to process is important. You are giving your nervous system a chance to deactivate. The breath is your clue that it is working]. If you go through these first four steps a few times, very slowly and you are still aware of the activation or even the "upset" inside you, go ahead with the next step.

5. Look around and count how many shades of brown, white or any predominant color you find nearby. Notice if you take a deeper breath. Let it happen.

6. If you need to, repeat these steps to increase your deactivation.

Keeping your nervous system calm helps your class to calm because you lend them your stability.

The Learning Zone

When a child is amped up and activated, he is not in the learning zone. In this condition, it is not possible for a child to learn. Telling a child to calm down, or stop fighting, or apologize, when the nervous system is not on the daisy petals only adds to the child's problem and creates further frustration for the teacher.

Save your energy and your breath. You can't correct these behaviors with words or reasoning. Instead, turn to a particular type of sensory experience to help the child to calm. Think of how we naturally calm babies. Rocking, cooing, cuddling, and shielding from bright lights are typical methods used to calm infants. As we grow, there are certain sensations that help us to calm and be in the learning zone. Children tend to find these sensory activities on their own. When we recognize a pattern, it helps us see what the child needs. We'll get into this more specifically in a little bit.

 **When a child is not in the learning zone, it is not possible for him to benefit from what you are saying.**

Trapped

Calmly catching a child's eyes with a look of love can open the door to conversation and help her to stay on the daisy petals. Your accepting presence and engagement with a child and your willingness to take time to meet the child in her world will go miles to bringing stability into her day.

When a child is already out of the learning zone and off the tip of the daisy petal, scolding or punishing him for disobedience will drive him further from the petal. If he's forced into a time out, away from the person who helps him stay on the petals, he feels isolated and rejected. Yet we often, unintentionally, get children into situations where they have no power and are overwhelmed. There is nothing quite so upsetting, actually traumatizing, as being trapped, like being sent to your room behind a closed door, or forced into a car seat when upset.

If the "trapped" feeling is frequently repeated, the child's nervous system learns to go into overload and fall off the tip of the daisy petal as a habit. This is what I call the well-worn rut. The child gets activated and shoots right through the zone of learning, off the end of the petal, and into overwhelm.

As they waited in line at the bank, Mom was holding her 3-year-old by the hand. The girl twisted and whined; "Let's go! Do we have to stay here?" The girl's voice became more high pitched, and her movements less controlled as she jerked at her mother's arm. Her little face paled and her eyes took on a desperate look to match her tone of voice.

Just then a lanky, young, dark-skinned woman asked if she

could watch the girl while Mom completed her banking. With mom's consent, our hero placed the child on the counter and spoke with her face-to-face. She asked about her day and told her what she was doing as she filled in her own deposit slip. The child's voice dropped from its high pitch. Her shoulders lowered and she began to gaze around the bank. Seeing her mother, a smile graced the child's face and she made eye contact with the kind, dark-skinned woman again. Mom was soon by her daughter's side. After smiling thank yous, Mom and daughter walked out of the bank together.

The caring interaction with our hero helped the child connect different parts of her brain. The safe social interaction also brought her attention away from being stuck in line and forced to do something upsetting. The change in this girl's voice was a neurological response. Her nervous system was saying, "I'm out of here," and taking her whole body along for the ride. This girl was not being willful and obstinate. She was genuinely past what she could tolerate and about to melt into a puddle of emotional overload.

When a child is "losing control," her state is likely neurological in origin. By changing what her sensory system receives, we can get help her get back onto the daisy petal.

Easy conversation is a good way to make this transition. Slowing down and talking with a child gives him the chance to process what was overwhelming. He may be so overwhelmed that he is "frozen" and unable to talk. We'll get to a clearer understanding of becoming immobile in chapter 12. For now, simply think of meeting the child where he is. Nonverbal communication is strong communication. A loving look, a gentle accepting touch, or a gesture to indicate we are leaving can be reassuring when a child is in overload.

Sensation connects directly to the "emotional feeling" part of our brains. Thus, we often stay on the daisy petals,- in the learning zone, - through sensory experiences. The next chapter will help us understand how that works.

Crazy Eight

Most of us have a good personal understanding of the five senses – seeing, hearing, smelling, tasting & the sense of touch.

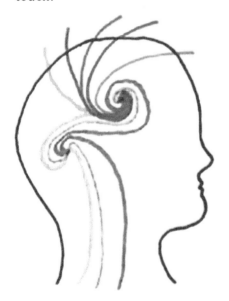

There are three more senses that are especially important for teachers of young children.

Ear Balance: (originating in the inner ear):

Our sense of movement is stimulated whenever our head moves. Whether we are jumping, going down a slide, swinging, running, rolling, spinning, rocking, or just shaking our head, ear balance is at work. In fact, ear balance is a major contributor to physical balance in our bodies.

Body position: (originating in muscles, joints and tendons): We use our sense of body position when we are hugged, or are bumped into. Hanging from a bar, the pressure of a headband or hat, even a belt around the waist; each provides a sense of body position. The awareness of our body and its parts supports good coordination and athletic ability and interrelates with all of our other senses. For example: seeing, moving our heads (stimulating ear balance) and the sense of body position, combine to give us balance.

The sense of our body's position, more than any other sense, tends to help us stay on the petals. You are invited to a free training at https://www.lethamarchetti.com/freetraining for more information on using body position to increase self-control.

Organ sense: (awareness of our heart's beat, digestion, need to use the bathroom, etc.)

Our brains have 500 million nerve endings in the gastrointestinal system or "gut". That's a lot of communication with the emotional center in our brain. Some children are very sensitive to this. When they digest they stop in their tracks. Some are frightened by a racing heartbeat. Some children don't pick up on this sense very easily and by the time they realize they need to go to the bathroom it's too late.

These eight senses are crucial to helping children stay in the learning zone. Have you ever noticed how reading a book and turning it slowly to show the pictures to your circle tends to bring calm to the group? You are working with the children's nervous systems in a way that helps them stabilize. You are bringing them into the learning zone.

The eyes directly connect the "feeling" brain (with its emotions) to the thinking brain. This puts things together neurologically for children. Sometimes, simply looking around the room, taking in what he sees, is enough to keep a child going around the daisy petals. This trains his or her system into a mature pattern, activating and deactivating, petal after petal, which is our goal.

Yes, this is why some children look around the room a lot. Rather than being distracted, their systems are trying, naturally, to be on the daisy petals. The outdated idea of correcting the child for being "distractible" is updated thanks to our understanding that once the child is ready, he will focus on the task and learning can take place. Imagine a child's nervous system, trying to deactivate while a teacher continues giving more instructions to look forward, listen, pay attention, etc. The nervous system is likely to be overloaded and the child will likely have a melt down or go into a freeze.

Sound is stabilizing for some children. Do you have children who make noises as they play? Maybe you've seen cute videos of babies recognizing their special songs and going from a bundle of upset to smiling, wiggling delight. These are children for whom sound is a primary means of staying on the petals.

Smell takes many comforting forms. The blanket full of drool that stinks to most people, may mean things are okay to its owner. That certain scent of Mom or the smell of a favorite food can add order to a nervous system that has activated right off the petals.

Does that thumb really taste good?

Who doesn't love a favorite meal? It can calm a tough day.

Taste and the whole oral area are very useful for calming the nervous system. The comfort associated with sucking has been a major part of your children's lives.

Maybe Mom wants that pacifier taken away and when you do, you notice Gavin is more activated and less easily calmed.

An interesting thing about sensation is that it has to be just right. If we are replacing something that is unacceptable with a more appropriate activity, we need to replicate the sensation as closely as we can to be successful.

If Gavin is sucking, we need a chew toy that can be sucked. Often, the pacifier is simply held in the mouth, more like oral touch. Can such a need be met with musical toys like a kazoo, mouth harp, harmonica, and so on?

You may be able to calm some dragon-like behavior in your classroom by providing oral sensation. When you see her sucking her shirt, consider a chewy stick or aquarium tubing tied into a necklace. Other chewable accessories include Ps & Qs and Chewelry. You can find many options on the web.

❖   ❖   ❖

Touch Down!

A loving touch, a gentle stroke, a hand caressing a child's head; these have an effect on the nervous system. Some children are very sensitive to touch — either liking it or hating it. When the child likes it, it helps him stay on the petals. You can use it to support the child to calm. When the child hates it, call an occupational therapist in and find another sense that helps this child calm. Blaine is an example of a child who is overly sensitive to a certain type of touch.

> *Blaine comes through the door with a jump. He tosses his pack towards his cubby. When it hits the divider he picks it up and tries again. "Slam," it lands. Seeing the beanbag pillow, he takes off running and lands with a roll, barely on the giant pillow. "That was fun!" Blaine exclaims as he grabs at his crotch. Blaine gets up and jumps on the pillow again. He grabs at his crotch, finds a blanket and some stuffed animals, dumps them on the pillow, grabs at his crotch again, and prepares for another crash landing. When asked, his response is always, "No, I don't have to pee."*

It turns out Blaine "used to be" sensitive to clothing — like tags and seams. At my suggestion, he started wearing underwear without tags or seams and marvelously, his frequent grabbing at his crotch went away. Blaine's underwear was irritating him. This meant he was nearly always teetering at the tip of his daisy petal. It meant that he could not fully deactivate at school. Once the irritant was removed, therapy progressed more quickly and the classroom was less challenging for Blaine.

❖   ❖   ❖

Rock 'n Roll

Have you had Rocking Rosie in your room? She is not rocking to distract others or to get attention. She is feeding her nervous system, helping it to calm, as it calmed when she was in the womb and she experienced rocking whenever Mom moved. When the nervous system is stabilized (on the daisy petals), it's ready to learn. Her system is supporting her so she can learn.

You can help Rosie by providing lots of opportunities for her to rock safely. You might offer a swing, rocking chair, hammock, or simply a chance to play a game involving sitting and rocking with control. Dancing is also a great way to allow spontaneous rocking and moving. The child will do what her system craves, the fancy neurons will fire, and she can be in the learning zone.

Rocking side to side stimulates different parts of our ear balance than rocking front to back. The system knows what it needs. As we watch and think about what might support a child, we need to replicate the sensation he or she is seeking as closely as we can in order to be successful. Jumping stimulates the movement sense in our inner ears. But it's not the same type of movement as rocking.

❖　❖　❖

Snuggle Bear

Samantha arrives at the "Bears" room with a wide-eyed look, mismatched socks, and hair flying. As usual, Mom is in a hurry. Emma notices Mom sign Samantha in and make an exit without saying hello or helping Samantha to settle.

With her coat still on Samantha goes over to teacher Emma and snuggles into a place between Emma and the edge of the couch. Emma suggests Samantha take her coat off. Samantha just shakes her head and burrows into the space she has made.

Samantha feels safe between Emma and the couch. Her brain

is getting lots of information that calms the upset of getting to school.

The weight of her coat with its belt around her waist, the pressure of Emma's body on one side, and the feeling of the couch on the other side are helpful to Samantha. They let her know where her body is. It's like a hug. She is naturally getting the body input that she needs.

The benefit is due to her sense of where her body is. Being squeezed is like a big hug to her nervous system. It lets her know she is here and safe. This body sense is the same one that prompts some children to do full body slams into walls and couches and to fall frequently for what looks like no reason. In such cases, the subconscious brain is driving behavior. Trying to overcome it with thought processes won't be helpful. Instead, we need to learn the body's unspoken language and respond to the needs it's expressing.

The language of the nervous system is sensation.

The right sensations help children to be in the learning zone.

That Takes Guts!

Sarah had been jumping around on the mini trampoline. Suddenly she stops in her tracks in front of teacher Aaron. She looks as if something is wrong. He hears her digestion. She stops, wondering if something is wrong, yet stays mute. Aaron waits as her system calms. He knows she is activated. "Do you feel your tummy?" he asks. "That's OK." As the sensation of something inside her moving is met with Aaron's stability, Sarah calms.

For Sarah, her organ sense was overwhelming. While digestion is a normal response to her activity, to Sarah it's a big sensation. A simple part of daily living is too much for her developing system. Aaron wisely let her know she was fine and with his presence, helped her calm.

Each type of sensory input has the potential to push a child into feeling overwhelmed (as was Sarah's experience) or to help support a child toward the zone of learning.

Jason is a round boy. Yesterday, in the school garden, Jason was sampling the different plants. He just finished his own lunch and now he's asking if he can have Harold's apple. Jason sits and devours Harold's apple bite after bite. At home, Jason asks for food right before bedtime.

No part of Jason's lunch goes uneaten because there is something about the weight of a full belly that comforts him and helps him stay on the daisy petals. A full tummy is a big sensory input affirming his comfort before he drifts off to sleep.

Doggone Good

Pets, especially dogs and lap cats, bring their stability in a contagious way. So much better than any stuffed animal, a well-trained dog or cuddly cat responds to a child, setting up a very appealing and encouraging social interaction. A dog will not tell a child what to do, or speak in a language that's confusing. Thus, shy children can find an entrée to socialization through the work of our furry four-footed friends.

Children subconsciously communicate with mammals in a manner that supports development and helps them to stay in the learning zone. This is especially important for children who are newly placed in daycare or are in a new school. In these instances,

children typically need more support to adjust and settle. Young children who are non-verbal can have positive interactions with a well-trained pet. It helps them calm and sets up their developing nervous systems to mature successfully.

A gentle, patient dog that enjoys being touched can add valued stability in daycare. I've even seen little jumpy Chihuahuas make a substantial difference. The key is that the dog be calmer than the person who needs support. Having a more regulated nervous system than the child, means the dog has something to offer.

How We Develop

We are going to use our hands to learn what a neuron is like.

Point your finger, like this, with Dr. Dani (who lent us her arm for these pictures.)

If we let the pointing finger represent the part of the nerve that receives touch information, then we can allow the hand to represent the cell body. The elbow plays the part of a neuron connecting to another neuron, muscle, or something else.

Touch

It's an amazing thing.

If something like a mosquito touched our nerve model at the tip of your finger, a signal would be sent to the cell body (the hand.) The cell body would send this important signal (down the arm toward the elbow) to its destination. This is how a typical neuron in your body works. A stimulus comes in and the cell body sends it on. The "sending it on" (down the arm, in our model) is the important thing.

Now we'll make a model of a neuron in the brain.

The brain has some fancy neurons.
They get information from more than one type of sense at once. Our first model only had the sense of touch. In this model, five

different senses are coming into one cell body. Please go ahead and open your hand like this with Dr. Dani. You'll understand why after we finish the exercise.

What makes this really important for us is that each of these five senses, represented by our fingers, must converge at once on the cell body for the information to be sent down the line. In this model, the information is sent from the hand to the elbow. Learning is the sending along of this sensory information.

This is really important.
Several senses have to be in use at the same time for us to learn. (My hand model has five. It could be less. It is often more.)

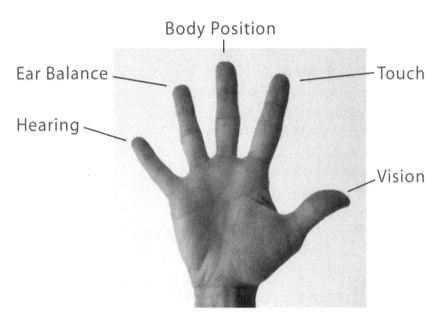

Even as adults, we learn the same way. Now you know why I had you tracing petals with your finger, moving around, and pointing. I added body position, touch and even ear balance to what you were taking in. I did this so that you would grab hold of the daisy petal concept (activation/deactivation) and I knew that if I brought in as many senses as possible, your fancy brain neurons would be most likely to complete their tasks and you would learn.

This is how people learn – by receiving lots of different types of sensory input at the same time. In fact, we don't learn without moving. So, if you didn't "do" the activities I've already mentioned in this book, I invite you to go back and have some fun. As you do them, their rationale has a chance to become a part of you. This makes it easier for the information to be readily available when you need it. For instance, if you perform my hand model, each time you look at your open hand you can be reminded that we learn when several senses come into play at the same time.

Let's apply this to young children.

> *Mario is learning shapes. As he squirms in his seat he keeps looking out the window and kicking his legs. "Cir-cle... cir-cle... cir-cle," he mutters as he sticks the round segments of a caterpillar on a page. Mario starts to rock his chair from side to side. Teacher Grace hears the "chunk, chunk, chunk, chunk" of Mario's chair legs hitting the floor. She thinks, "I tell him almost every day not to do this. He's at it again!"*

Let's see how many types of sensory input we can find in Mario's experience.

> Sight
> Sound
> Touch
> Body Position
> Ear Balance

If a neuron had the first four senses (sight, sound, touch, and body position) reaching it but, in order to do its job, it needed ear balance too, it would send a subconscious signal to get it. Something like, "Can I have some head movement here? I really want to learn this, and I could send this info along, if I just had some ear balance input. Mario, help me out here!"

This sort of demand, from a place deep in the brain, drives a lot of behavior that makes adults uncomfortable. No wonder behavior can be baffling! Sometimes we don't see what's causing it at all.

When we see children jumping, spinning, rocking, and doing so many other behaviors instead of just sitting still, it's a good guess that their little systems are requiring the movement to support their development.

This does not mean we should let children run wild, fulfilling their inner drives. It means, instead, that we should support them by helping them to find an acceptable version of whatever it is they are craving.

When Celeste has to throw things, telling her she is not allowed to throw does not allow her system to develop. We actually want her to get to the point where she doesn't need to throw things. To help her do that, we find appropriate, acceptable throwing activities:

Can you get the toy to land in the basket?

What if I move the basket further away?

Is this beanbag better for throwing? How about that rag ball?

Make it a game. Try throwing in an arc, under one leg, facing the other way, two at a time, standing sideways... She will find the variations that suit her.

For Mario, if he needs to rock, let's get something in the room to meet that need. Below is a balance board. With a foot on either side, he can stand and rock.

Mom says, "Hui loves to jump and crash into pillows. It's as if 'No Fear' is his motto. He pulls the cushions off the couch and jumps into them, even though I tell him we don't do that in our home."

The teachers have to keep a close eye on him because he jumps off the play equipment where there is not a big pile of pillows to catch him.

Let's look at this. Hui loves to jump and crash. I call him a crash and burn boy. He needs to jump. What type of jumping or jumping equipment is safe and acceptable?

Trampoline
Crash pad
Jumping over lines in the cement
Jumping along a pathway on the rug
Hopscotch
Jump rope
Jumping from the stump into the sawdust pile
and more...

Giving Hui's neurons what they need, will decrease his need to jump and crash.

There are at least two things going on when children display a need for sensory input.

1. Sensation can help calm or regulate the system. We saw this in the chapter called Crazy Eight when we looked at different types of senses. Sometimes sensory input is calming. Sometimes it's irritating. You will recognize which is happening.

2. For whatever reason, a child may need input of a specific type to help learning take place.

Children gravitate toward the sensory input they need.

Help them get it in a safe, acceptable manner.

This is an especially helpful principle. We don't have to guess. Children show us what they need. We can shape it, make it safe, and have fun in the process.

Earlier we looked at Jason who likes to have a full belly. He likes to chew, too. The questions I ask as a therapist are: What can he chew on? What is safe that Mom allows and will meet his needs? Celery, dried fruit, and gum are great for chewing. Apples, carrots, or water will add weight to the stomach. Providing these things and watching to see which ones are "winners" can help Jason be capable and in the learning zone. He doesn't have to be told to do something, or not do something. He'll respond positively to what helps.

Sensation: Friend or Foe?

O ne child is calmed with a gentle back rub. Another shrinks away, clearly perceiving the touch as unpleasant.

Jason and Salim play with trucks, pushing them around the yard. "Vrrrrr, vrrrr," they rumble around in a circle. Zoe stands like a statue with her hands over her ears.

As you think through your sensory system, you may recognize that one or more of your senses are extra sensitive. One at a time, imagine too much of each sense. If you find a sense that can more easily feel like too much to you than the others, you know some of what your children are going through. An example might be feeling carsick when your head moves a lot, because your ear balance is overly sensitive.

Sensory issues are common and frequently involve smell, taste, and touch. When the sensory issue limits your life, it's called a sensory processing disorder. Adults may have sensory processing disorders, but preschoolers are really too young to fit in this category. They are developing. In other words, as they grow and mature, they will hopefully get what they need so that a disorder does not develop. My goal as an occupational therapist is to help children develop successfully. Let's avoid a diagnosis that says they have a disorder, while they are still developing. We can give them more of what they need now, so they can build a solid neurological foundation that will support their development.

Zoe may complain about noise, but later the same day you may hear her yelling. Jason would rather take his shirt off, but sometimes he wears a heavy jacket. Such observable contradictions make working with sensory issues challenging. They reveal a need for an occupational therapist. You can find more information on my website: www.OccupationalTherapy-Letha.com. We can even have a consultation over the phone to tease out what's happening.

When a child's nervous system is the issue, a skilled occupational therapist uses sensation to help adjust that system. An occupational therapist may give you, and the parents, some tips or suggestions for activities during the day to help children deal with their over and/or under sensitivities.

There are two classic classroom solutions to help children with sensory issues: peace and quiet and body position sense input.

1. Peace and Quiet.
When a child is activated and ready to fall off the end of the daisy petal, you may see her seek out a quiet place, a corner where there is less sensory input. There are suggestions at the end of this book to help you make a quiet place.

Along this same line, take a look around your room, recall your own experience with a sensory issue, and imagine how children in the room with specific sensory sensitivities might feel. Peace from overstimulation is quiet to the senses. Let's look at them in more detail.

A. Vision: Is there a mass of visual overload? Are walls and windows covered with bright colorful items? Do things hang from the ceiling and move causing more visual stimulation? If so, a child who is easily overwhelmed visually will have great difficulty coming into the zone of learning. At the very least, have a large section of the room where visually sensitive children can go, any time, to rest from overwhelming stimulation. This does not mean we want to live in barren rooms with nothing on the walls. We just don't want the visual stimuli to be overwhelming.

B. Sound: Is there a continual noise in the room? Does a sound-sensitive child have a place where he can go and continue doing what everyone is doing, but also avoid the sensation that overwhelms him?

C. Smell: Does the classroom have inherent odors that some children find noxious? If shoes are taken off, are they placed away from where a sensitive child sits? Do lunch smells upset some children? Children can't just "get used" to the offence. If the nervous system of an odor-sensitive child is continually bombarded by smells, he or she will fall from the zone of learning, right off the daisy petal.

D. Taste: Is a child given food that she truly hates? If she is forced to eat it, she will not be able to stay in the zone of learning.

E. Touch: Children who are hypersensitive to touch are prone to coming unglued over the slightest touch. Sometimes a single hair brushing against their skin is too much. Placing the girl with big, curly hair next to the boy who can't tolerate light touch can bring on a fight if her hair touches his arm. Following is an example of specific sensory input being helpful.

> *Sasha carries a stuffed toy almost all the time. He is seldom far from his "blanky." He really likes its soft, satiny edge. During story time he strokes it's smooth edge as he settles into Teacher Joanie's lap.*

Sasha borrows Joanie's stability while enjoying the comfort that stroking the soft fur of his stuffed animal or the satin on his blanket brings to his nervous system.

Touch helps Sasha to fully calm, in other words, to come to the center of the daisy. This is crucial for development. When Sasha's system comes all the way back to center, completing activation and deactivation, his nervous system has done something mature. The nervous system likes to do a full cycle of activation and deactivation. Teacher Joanie helps Sasha form a pathway by supporting his sensory needs and allowing him to carry his animals, stroke his blanket, and cuddle in her lap. The more Sasha's young system can complete a cycle of activation and deactivation, the greater his ability to stay on the daisy petals.

Proper and timely sensation supports deactivation.

Full cycles of activation and deactivation are our goal.

These sorts of experiences (completing activation/deactivation cycles) early in life, set the child's neurological system up to handle stresses and challenges. The child comes to believe that he can take on difficult things and that when something seems challenging, he will succeed.

Developing the ability to stay on the daisy petals is what takes children on to maturity.

F. Organ Sense: For some children, a racing heart is overwhelming, for others the feelings of digestion, another organ sense, can be just too much.

Dillon proclaimed, "I need a rest!" and plopped down right next to me. I could feel his heart pounding. He hadn't been running long but to his little body, the activation level was very high. He was right. He needed a rest. He needed to deactivate.

When we carefully observe a child, we can notice what happened before she became overwhelmed, and

ideally even notice what happened before that. Careful noticing helps us to find ways to support the child to stay on the daisy petals.

The first sign that the child is going off the daisy petal is the time to provide the sensory input that helps the child deactivate.

G. Ear Balance Sense:

Will is wearing his tennis shoes that light up today. Michael and Nolan have them, too. As Will heads out to play with Nolan, he looks down at the threshold, holds onto the doorjamb and steps with caution. While Nolan climbs over the landscape border holding in the tan bark, Will sits on it. After a moment he gets up and goes to the play structure. He sits on the bottom step. His teacher has never seen him climb on it or sit on a swing. When class lines up, Will holds Teacher's hand as they walk back to the room.

Will is experiencing a snag in the development of the sense that's stimulated when his head moves, ear balance. Being off the ground is scary for him. Crossing from one surface to another, (like going from linoleum to cement) makes him uneasy. If he's pushed to move quickly, or do things that require him to be elevated above the ground he becomes overwhelmed. Walking on stairs is only possible with a hand to hold or a secure railing.

What makes things worse for Will are the thick-soled shoes he's wearing. He may as well be wearing ski boots for the amount of sensation that gets through his shoes to tell his body where he is. Something thin-soled, like moccasins, would be a better choice. Let's look at this in more detail.

2. Sensing Body Position

Can you imagine not knowing where your body is? The brain really dislikes that! In response, it will ask for sensory input so it can make connections and foster development. What does this body position sensory input look like? It looks like crashing into things, stomping, flapping arms, and generally being rougher than most adults think is necessary. Doing these things helps a child to increase the sense of where his body is.

Maggie jumps as she approaches the doorway of her classroom. The line builds behind her as teacher Joshua says, "Come on in Mary." She makes it through the doorway and puts her things in her cubby. Joshua asks, "Can we hop like kangaroos to the circle?" He starts an impromptu song, "We are happy kangaroos, hopping together, hopping together. We are happy kangaroos..."

Of all the types of sensory input, the sense of where one's body is in space tends to be the most helpful in keeping children on the petals.

Melt Downs and Freeze Ups

An activated nervous system that does not deactivate but keeps going (off the tip of the daisy petal, in our model), is in a survival response. This means part of the brain perceives this situation as a life or death matter. Beginning in infancy, an overwhelmed baby kicks and cries to get her needs met so she survives. If no one comes to her aid, she will not live. To babies, all overwhelm is a matter of life and death. As children learn to stay on the daisy petals, this all-consuming situation improves. It may seem silly to an adult, but to children the subconscious sense is that they are up against something that will kill them. This explains the dramatic responses we see.

In an overwhelmed state, all sorts of changes happen in the body to preserve life. Overwhelm is a subconscious state with no connection to the thinking mind. There are three possible responses: fight, flight, or freeze.

1. Fight

Subconscious feeling: "I can take this on and win!"

Fight looks like:

Physical fighting
Raising fists
Gnashing teeth
Swinging arms in disgust
Punching pillows
Kicking at the ground
Full-out tantrum (fighting against self)
Racing heart

Rapid breathing

A fight response can be one or more of the behaviors listed above. In its extreme, it reminds me of a dragon that is all teeth and claws.

This is the first big response when we are in an overwhelming situation.

Marcus can go almost five minutes on the playground before he gets into a fight. It's usually with the same boy. His teacher has become adept at keeping them apart. Still, there is a simmering anger in Marcus most of the time.

Marcus runs at a high activation level. It is as if he looks for things to fight about. There was a squabble over a ball. When Marcus got it back he waited a good ten minutes and then found the other boy, cornered him, and was ready to take his revenge when the teacher intervened. Marcus is a "take no prisoners" kind of guy.

Marcus' teacher's challenge is more than keeping her children safe. She needs to see the thing before the trigger that sets Marcus off. It might be the look in his eye or the set of his jaw, but whatever it is, it tells her he is activating. This is when the skilled teacher will intervene with another activity. Yes, she is distracting him. But most importantly, she is giving his nervous system the opportunity to deactivate. Once it starts down the rut of typical response, it's too late. When she changes his course early on, Marcus stays in the learning zone. Now that the teacher understands why redirecting Marcus to the tricycle track works, she is doing it more often. She is supporting Marcus to stay on the daisy petals so he doesn't behave like a dragon.

Between the teacher's good work, six months of occupational therapy in the clinic, and follow-through at home, Marcus has found new neurological pathways. He's calmer and his anger level is most often undetectable. He will do better with more treatment but already we see his nervous system learning to stay in the learning zone – on the petals.

2. Flight
Subconscious feeling: "I can't win this. I better get out of here!"

Flight typically looks like:

Running away
Leaving the room
Racing heart
Rapid breathing
Hiding

This is the nervous system's second option when we are in an overwhelming situation.

Liza has started to attend a new school. When Dad drops her off, she runs across the playground, away from everyone. As soon as it's yard time again, off she goes. The teachers are concerned because she has gotten out of the gate once already.

Liza's system chooses to get away from her overwhelmed feelings in order to lower her sensory input and stress level. She is not ready to take on this new group of people in unfamiliar surroundings. Flight can be a healthy way of coping as she gets used to the school. By getting away from the activity, there is less stimulation so she can gradually process and acclimate to her surroundings. If the teacher and her father pushed her to go inside, it would raise her stress level, making the transition more difficult for Liza. As her nervous system regulates and learns she is safe, running away will be replaced with a more appropriate response. With the right sensory support, as we saw in the last chapter, she'll get through this more easily and she won't need to run away.

3. Freeze
Subconscious feeling: "This is too much for me. I can't fight and win. I'm unable to get away. The best I can do play dead."

Freeze comes in degrees. It can look like all or some of these:

Eyes stuck in a vacant stare
Mouth open with lower lip slack

Body not moving or not able to move
Voice changing to high pitch, gravely, or gone altogether
Heart rate drops
Breathing slows
Looking like a statue - motionless

In it's full form, freeze is like a dragon in hibernation – the body minimizes functions and simulates death.

Freeze has degrees. We can be a little freezy or totally frozen.

Avoiding a Rut

Whatever over activated the child's system, the body is responding with a survival mechanism, like an opossum that plays dead. We may look at the situation and think it is nothing. But children are similar to adults in that what may upset one person, can make another laugh. What's nothing to you may be extremely significant to someone else – especially a child.

Now, lets look at this in light of a developing nervous system. Young children are not able to "stay on the daisy petals" without help. If they are repeatedly overwhelmed, their developing system learns to shoot right off the tip of the daisy petal.

There are two options here. The first is to fall off the petal or stay

on it.

We want to support children so they can stay on the petal – in the learning zone. This takes patience and repetition for all involved. Once the system starts the rhythm of staying on the petal; going round and round, as if tracing the outside of a daisy, it likes it better than falling off the end and behaving like a dragon. Generally, children don't like being out of control. They have no words to describe it and are relieved to leave dragon like behavior behind. They'd rather be on the petals.

The second option is which path the nervous system will choose if it goes off the tip of the daisy petal into the land of overwhelm. If it habitually chooses one particular path, a neurological pathway can develop. I call this the well-worn rut.

Pathways are being laid down very quickly during development (700 to 1,000 new connections per second in early development.) As activation starts, if it hits the well-worn rut, a physical response begins and it is very difficult to turn back. It's like driving onto the freeway on-ramp. Once you start down the ramp, you are going onto the freeway, and there's no turning back. Our nervous system is similar; it gets trained to a pattern and the response becomes habitual. For example, activation may consistently result in the fight response.

Do you know people whose frustration has a very short fuse and they seem to explode on whomever is around? Their friends and family become collateral damage from the shrapnel of their emotional explosions. After they blow up, the activation in their nervous systems is relieved and they feel like themselves. This relief reinforces the explosive response. (I blew up, now I feel better. So I learn to blow up to feel better.) Typically, the feeling of relief makes their explosion seem as if it's not a big deal. They wonder why the action that brought them relief seems so bad to someone else. This can be helped with therapy. Better yet, we can avoid developing this rut in a child's system.

Angela had a difficult birth. She arrived early at 32 weeks and needed medical support in the NICU. Mom also needed medical support and was not able to be with Angela for the first two days after her birth.

Angela had IVs, tubes, and wires all over her little body. It seemed every time someone touched her it was another sensory assault; bright lights, a jab, something pinching, or a tug at her arm, nose, or mouth.

Because a baby cannot fight or run away, she learns to "check out." It's the infant version of freeze. If support doesn't come in the form of a stable caregiver to help the child stay on the daisy petals, the child starts a pattern of being overwhelmed and going into freeze.

Angela became sensitive to light and touch and had eating issues. Her early transitions were mostly noxious. When she got to preschool, just entering the classroom was enough to take her to freeze. Her system was not able to process all the stimulation so it backed up like traffic on the freeway. Every time someone told her to hurry up, or move out of the doorway, it was more information to process. Since she was already overloaded, this "helpful" advice was anything but helpful.

To help a child in freeze, don't add more stimulation. Let her be and her system will catch up. Then she'll be ready to go forward. If the child is pushed and prodded when in freeze, it deepens the freeze and the rut. What we want is for the child to build an ability to handle more input and stay on the daisy petals. We need to support the child in being able to go round and round the daisy instead of flying off into overwhelm.

A child whose nervous system takes him or her into freeze easily, needs a slow pace. Think s l o w motion. When the child is ready to speed up, she will. By going very slowly the system learns to process the sensory world. A foundation is being established. We need a solid foundation to build a capable life.

A Safe Landing

As the child learns to activate and deactivate, it's crucial that deactivation is complete. As the nervous system calms fully, it gains the ability to do it again.

Rainier takes his shoes off as he comes through the door. Going directly to Teacher Quinton he asks for the trucks to play with. As Quinton goes to the closet to get the container of trucks, two other children arrive. One of their parents has a question for Quinton. While Quinton speaks with the parent,

Rainier is impatiently jumping and looking longingly toward the closet. Another interruption, and Rainier heads to the reading corner, looking for his favorite book.

Two minutes later, Quinton is free. He goes to Rainier, now kicking in frustration at the bookshelf. "I CAN'T FIND THE BIG FISH BOOK!" he yells. "Where are the TRUCKS?"

Quinton knows the importance of helping Rainier complete his cycle of activation and deactivation by fully calming down – coming back to the center of the daisy in our model. It is likely that simply providing Rainier with the bin of trucks will mean his activation increases – off the daisy petal.

Quinton sits with Rainier. "It's hard to wait. I'm sorry it took a while. Let's find your big fish book!"

Talking with Rainier and getting him to move his eyes and head connects different parts of the brain and helps with deactivation. Quinton's work was successful. Rainier's racing heart rate dropped. His body let go of its "ready to kick" attitude. A big breath came out and Rainier settled as Quinton found his favorite book. Looking at the pictures and talking with Quinton about them made it possible for Rainer's nervous system to deactivate. In our daisy model, this means going from the tip of a daisy petal back toward the center. Quinton wanted a "safe landing" for Rainier's frustrated emotions. To create one, he took time as they went through the book. He asked about illustrations and if Rainier has ever seen a real fish, up close. He spent a little longer in the calm place than Rainier had spent in the very frustrated place.

This helped Rainier's nervous system make helpful transitions and get solidly into the learning zone. When he went to play with the trucks, Rainier was able to play well with Logan.

When children are set up to succeed, the classroom can function as it was designed, to be a laboratory of learning.

On Alert: The Hypervigilant Child

Freckle-faced, red headed Tristan, in his green plaid shirt and dark grey cargo shorts is standing, looking out the window. Teacher Marie invites the class to look at a caterpillar. Tristan sees the stark, glaring reflection off the windshield of a passing car and doesn't seem to hear Marie at all. As the car drives off, the room's air conditioning unit kicks on. Tristan interrupts the class with a loud, "What's that?"

Marie draws him toward the activity. "Tristan, we have a furry caterpillar!" she says. Tristan looks at another child entering the room, seemingly unaware again of his teacher.

"Come, see!" Marie invites him warmly. Tristan's eyes follow Nathan, as he walks toward the group watching the caterpillar.

Tristan makes his way over and just as he is about to get close enough to see the crawling, woolly wonder for himself, Jeannie pushes Amanda so she can get closer. Amanda whines, "Stop it," and Tristan watches the girls. His progress towards Mr. Caterpillar has halted.

Marie looks to her assistant to help Tristan engage. This movement, also, seems to be of more interest to Tristan than the lesson she is offering.

Tristan has an acute awareness of his surroundings. He's always noticing, vigilant, like a lookout; making sure things are OK.

Here is a quote I especially like:

> *"...every child enters the classroom in a vehicle propelled by that child alone, at a particular pace and for a particular purpose"* - Vivian Gussin Paley
>
> [Quoted from: The Boy Who Would Be a Helicopter, Paley 1990, p. xii]

Tristan's "vehicle" has super sensitive detectors for anything new. He is hypervigilant. His alert system is over-the-top.

The brain has a couple of areas that specialize in early warning. When they are stimulated, Tristan doesn't feel safe. His body uses all its ability to notice things, to alert him and to protect him. To Tristan's brain, hearing Maria is not important. She needs to hear him; unknown danger is lurking.

You can imagine it this way. There are two lookouts in the brain. When the body finds itself in a transition, the lookouts notify the rest of the body; "Something has changed. There could be danger. Activate the nervous system!" To some degree the heart picks up pace, sending blood to the muscles that are preparing for action. Since Tristan is hypervigilant, he tends not to calm all the way down (in our model, back to the center of the daisy). This means he is still on the edge of high alert.

Children who live in this place tend to go off the end of the daisy petals with each transition. These transitions don't have to be as substantial as leaving the building. They can be as simple as moving over a change in the floor covering (linoleum to carpet) or changing activities (reading to coloring.)

It's these two lookouts, highly active in a developing brain that hasn't yet learned to deactivate, that are responsible for challenges in the classroom during transitions.

When Tristan is in a new place, he asks question after question; "What's behind that door... What is this for?" When he goes somewhere new he looks the place over thoroughly; he looks into cabinets and behind doors. He can't settle until he is familiar with the new area. His brain is demanding information because its deep "alert" centers are stimulated even more in a new environment.

Marie used to think she couldn't catch Tristan's attention. Once she learned that he was hypervigilant, she knew how to help him.

"Tristan, what do you see?" asked Marie.

"The light is flickering Teacher Marie."

Slowly, she responds, "Yes, look at that! The light is flickering. It's brighter, then it's almost off. Now it's brighter. It's still flickering. That light flickers."

Teacher Marie is making a space for Tristan to explore his environment. The eyes have a good relationship with the lookouts. They take in information and send it directly to the two lookouts and the thinking part of the brain. The thinking part (we can call this high command), with Marie's help, is accepting that the lights are flickering. There is no judgment (good or bad); there is simply an acceptance of reality. High command lets the lookouts know the nervous system doesn't have to be on high alert.

Marie wants to help Tristan settle all the way down, to develop the ability to calm himself. So she takes time to let him settle. They talk about lights.

"Tristan, what different lights are in this classroom?"

"There's a light over the terrarium," offers Tristan. "There are six lights hanging from the ceiling," he elaborates. "There is a little red light on the music player."

Tristan even found the light on the surge protector between Marie's desk and the wall. Because this seemed to take extra vigilance, the last find made Marie wonder if he needed more time to fully deactivate, so she raised a question for discussion. "Does the skylight count as a light?" A few minutes later, Tristan was sitting in circle, ready for story time.

The lookouts were satisfied. High Command was able to help more because there was social chatting. Talking via an easy, curious interchange helps High Command send calming messages to the lookouts. For many years, we've thought of this as distraction. In a sense, it is. But the real benefit is in bringing the various centers of the brain into action. With casual, social chatting, the lookouts aren't the only game in town and they work with the rest of the brain instead of trying to run the whole body.

To deepen Tristan's deactivation, Marie could have had Tristan breathe out his name. (You can find this activity in the companion book, *Dragons & Daisies: Preschool Fun and Games).*

 **Support hypervigilant children to calm by having them look around and chat – like playing "I Spy."**

The Scots, way back when, came up with a little prayer that so typifies a child's view:

> *From ghoulies and ghosties*
> *And long-leggedy beasties*
> *And things that go bump in the night,*
> *Good Lord, deliver us!*

When a child continually looks for issues and problems, the nervous system cannot rest. This is a rut worth getting out of. Get more ideas on getting out of and avoiding ruts from a free training for those who purchase this book. Access this extra help at https://www.lethamarchetti.com/freetraining.

She's Demanding Attention Because She Needs It

When a childcare professional asked me about attention-getting behavior I told her the child was demanding attention because she needed it.

"Well, obviously!" intoned Grace.

"Look at it like this," I responded. "Shirley wants attention because she is unsettled inside. She tries to deactivate and is not successful. Getting adult attention has worked for her in the past. If you try to get her to do something by herself, her neurological need is still unmet. On the other hand, if you lavish her with attention. You'll feed her nervous system. She will get back on the daisy petals, learn to stay there for longer periods, and she'll be able to go on with life."

Grace looked at me with squinty eyes and a questioning tilt to her head. "Shirley can never get enough attention. She always wants more!"

"Grace," I said, "If you were thirsty and no one would give you more than a few drops of water, you'd still be thirsty. Shirley is not getting what she needs. When she gets enough attention, she will no longer demand it. Eventually, her nervous system will get what it's been craving. The need will be met."

"Wow! That is so simple!" replied Grace, now calm and smiling.

Sometimes we look at behavior in terms of a pattern that we want to encourage or discourage. It's important to remember that young children are developing. So there is change and growth. Neurologically motivated behavior needs proper neurological input.

 **Lavishing attention on a child who craves it will help her develop past needing continual attention.**

There is no substitute for professional help when it's needed. While people wait, hoping their child will outgrow issues, neural pathways are being laid down. The longer we wait, the harder it is to build pathways that keep us on the daisy petals and the more therapy is needed in years to come.

When your child sees an occupational therapist, also referred to as an OT, he or she will likely recommend activities for school as part of treatment. We sometimes call this a sensory diet.

I guess every OT has his or her particular prescription for the proper amount of sensory stimulation. Here is mine. It is a general guideline, a starting point, which I adjust for each child, as needed.

R̶x **Occupational Therapy Prescription:**

Every Waking Hour Provide 10 minutes of

_____

(The activities in the blank will nearly always be what the child gravitates toward.)

For example: The girl who is pulling and twisting her hair can have a doll with long hair or thin ribbons tied to a clip to touch and enjoy.

The boy who bounces and jumps spontaneously and frequently can have jumping activities like a mini trampoline, hopscotch, jumping from letter to letter on the rug...

The child who rocks his chair can be set up with a safe rocker board, a swing, or a seesaw.

The child who spins can play with sit-n-spin or spin while hanging on a trapeze.

The boy who chews his shirt can be given dried fruit, jerky, and maybe gum at home.

As you've read earlier, simultaneous, multisensory input is generally the most helpful.

You may have a clear idea of the child's need. Sharing this information with a parent may be enough to bring about positive change. It is really great if the parent(s) call in an occupational therapist as well so their child can have additional support for greater progress.

Now you have the concept. But here's the thing, ten minutes of prescribed activity every hour in an early childhood classroom is not possible. Something will get in the way; lunchtime, field outings, or other children who need attention. It just doesn't always work. An hour is sure to be missed. Some days, two hours will be missed. That is okay. You don't need to make up for what you missed. Just carry on in the next hour. What we are after is giving plenty of good sensory food to the nervous system.

What's a Teacher to Do?

Picture people who unbend paperclips while they listen in a meeting, chew on pens for oral sensation, or bounce one leg as they sit at the table. For some people, fidgeting provides the sensation their bodies require to stay on the daisy petals.

A wide variety of items are available to meet the need to fidget. Conveniently, they are called fidgets. Fidgets are extremely useful tools in the early childhood education classroom. Fidgets stimulate the senses. There are visual fidgets like kaleidoscopes; auditory fidgets like slide whistles; tactile fidgets like Koosh balls; smell fidgets like pouches of lavender; taste fidgets like Smarties; and oral fidgets like Ps & Qs. The list is endless.

Many classrooms have found that having a basket of fidgets available for children to use at will is beneficial.

Miss Harding met me at the door of her classroom. "Mike is in the blue, superman t-shirt. So far this year he hasn't been able to sit through story circle, successfully, even once."

Mike wandered from the Lego table to the kitchen area. "We're going to story circle," said Miss Harding as she led her class in a follow-the-leader ritual to the story corner.

Mike went back to the Lego table. Miss Harding took a basket of fidgets and passed it around the group. Mike arrived at the basket, eyeing the pink finger springs (coiled shoe laces), the tongue depressors wrapped with red and yellow pipe cleaners, and the spaghetti balls. There, underneath the squishy balloons with cornstarch inside, was something he wanted. Mike snatched up a key ring with several beads on it. He began to push them along and turn them. He put a finger through the ring and then two fingers. He kept playing with the fidget as he sat down.

As Miss Harding read, Mike made the beads go around one way, then another way. He spun them in place. He did not look up at Miss Harding once.

When Miss Harding finished the book she asked where the brave monkey pirate went. Mike's hand shot up as he said, "To the restaurant."

"Did he go anywhere else?" asked Miss Harding. "Yes," Mike quickly answered. "And the doctor."

It surely didn't look as if Mike was paying attention to Miss Harding. But, using the fidget helped Mike stay in the group and listen. He was able to stay in the learning zone.

Here is the challenge. Adding something new draws attention. Some children will throw the fidget. Some will want to play with it and with the child sitting nearby. This is when many teachers give up on fidgets. This is also when it is useful to remember Mike. He didn't seem to be paying attention, but he was. His nervous system was helped substantially by having sensory stimulation. It got his fancy, multi sensory neurons firing.

Typically, it takes a couple weeks for the novelty of fidgets to wear off. Children who benefit from using fidgets will still take them from a readily available basket. Those for whom fidgets have no appeal typically leave them alone. Gradually, the group settles according to its need. I encourage teachers to stay with the concept. Remember the idea that we must move to learn, and fidgets will become more "acceptable."

 ## Teachers do so much. They aren't therapists, too. Get help.

Children don't outgrow developmental issues as a matter of time alone. They must develop past them. This requires knowledgeable support. Too often, children get "stuck." Getting through an awkward time in development, without suffering from bullying or becoming a social outcast is important for a child's future success. Professional help can make all the difference. You can let parents know that occupational therapists work with developing children. They help them to get through challenges to a sense of capability. A recommendation for an occupational therapist is often pivotal, positively affecting the rest of a child's life.

No parent wants to hear that a caregiver thinks there is "something wrong" with his or her child. One way to open the conversation without being the "bad guy" is to tell parents you found a great website that talks about child development. You might be able to say you even saw "that thing" their child does mentioned and they might find it helpful to check out the Baffling Behavior Expert at: www.OccupationalTherapy-Letha.com.

No doubt the parents will thank you for caring and sharing your expertise.

My training site, for teachers and parents who are interested in gaining a deeper understanding of development and sensation, is www.LethaMarchetti.com. In addition to the free training, it offers a community for learning and supportive information.

You already know what you are after, getting to and staying in the learning zone. Here's a way to remember the basics:

The key to utilizing this book is

U.P.S.Y-DAISY

A phrase often used to reassure a small child while he or she is being lifted up.

U - Understand the child's experience

Ignore your own preconceived ideas for a few minutes and see through the child's experience. He is doing all he can to communicate with you. Take time, putting all else aside, to understand and honor what the child is telling you.

P - Petals are the place to stay

The petals of a daisy represent the learning zone. Tracing from the base of a petal to its tip represents activation in the nervous system. Tracing back toward the center represents deactivation. When a child's activation takes him off the petal, he is out of control, and unable to learn. Maturity is when we activate toward the tip of the petal and return fully to the center in cycle after cycle of activation and deactivation. Help children stay on the petals and in the learning zone.

S - Support with proper Sensation

Sensation is what helps us stay on the petals, in the learning zone. Adjusting the child's environment to match her sensory needs helps her stay on the petals. This may mean limiting sensory input or adding it.

Y - Take care of Yourself

When you are calm and stable, children borrow your stability. Your mature ability to activate and deactivate, as if you are tracing round and round on a daisy, shows children how to do the same. You are positively contagious!

Tips for Transitions

1. Get moving

2. Move your head or move a foot or move anything

3. You guessed it! Move

If you are sitting, stand up, and look around.

Ask your class to find something like:
- Three different shades of blue
- A very smooth texture in the room
- A very rough texture in the room

Who can stand on all fours?

Can we balance on three?

How about two?

Can anyone balance on one foot?

Use music – Sing as you go to the next activity. You can make it up as you go:

We are all going (clap), to the lunch table (clap), to the lunch table (clap), to the lunch table. We are all going (clap) to the lunch table... Now, we are here!

Use chants:

1, 2, 3 Who wants to go with me?

1, 2, 3 Who wants to go with me?

1, 2, 3 Who wants to go with me?

Here we go, all in a row.

An Internet search for chants for children shows rich resources available for free online as well as books of helpful chants.

Assign children an animal behavior as they go:

Jory, you may hop like a bunny to the door.

Macey, you may crawl like a cat to the door.

Simon, you may walk like a raccoon to the door.

For more activities, get my companion book ***Dragons & Daisies: Preschool Fun and Games.*** It offers activities for easily over-whelmed children and group activities to help young children stay on the daisy petals.

A Quiet Place

Many children need a place to which they can retreat and feel safe.

> *Daniel arrived early and went right to the block bin. Justin and Bryce came in and picked up blocks, too. Justin took one that Daniel was just about to add to his structure. Bryce came through with a dinosaur and inadvertently knocked over part of Daniel's tower. Just then the teacher told the class to come to circle time. Bryce turned around, just brushing the tower and Daniel's creation crashed down. Daniel heard his teacher's next call as painfully loud.*
>
> *Instead of going to the circle, Daniel went to the cubbyhole. Moving pillows and pulling a heavy blanket over himself, he took a deep breath. Daniel looked out into the main classroom through strips of cloth. One piece, in particular, perfectly blocked his view of Bryce.*
>
> *Daniel stayed hidden for several minutes, watching and listening as Teacher Jessica told the group; today is Monday. Justin got to stick "Monday" on the wall. Daniel got up and went to the circle.*

An overwhelmed nervous system can find relief when it's allowed to escape the stress of so much sensory stimulation. Daniel understood that Bryce didn't mean to knock over his tower and Justin didn't mean to take his block. Still, he felt out of sorts. Mental comprehension isn't adequate. The body has to find a way to deal with the stress it holds. Daniel was activated enough that his hearing became hypersensitive.

The cubbyhole allowed Daniel to deactivate. Jessica knew Daniel would come out when he was ready. She was glad he took the initiative and found a way to settle. Jessica also understood that forcing a child to do something he is not yet ready for, only adds activation to the whole group. If this happens, someone is bound to fall off the daisy petal.

There are many ways to create a cozy cubbyhole. Here are some inventive examples I've seen.

Furniture for the classroom designed to include a round tube that a child can climb into. The other side has a clear, concave, plastic "bubble".

When cabinets are built close to the floor, two or more cabinet doors may be removed. The space is then fitted with pillows, blankets, and even stuffed animals. Some preschools staple sheer fabric or fabric strips over parts of the opening.

Put up a pup tent. There are lots of variations of pup tents. Some look like fire trucks, school buses, or castles.

A small playhouse can work well.

My favorite is to get a big appliance box, decorate it. (Glue on construction paper shapes, use markers, paint it, put stickers on it, etc.) Cut out doors and windows. Put some "pillow furniture" inside and it's good to go! Maybe the children make it into a house, a truck, or a cave — anything goes. It can be used inside and out. It takes on a life of its own as children drag it, dismember it, repurpose its parts, and eventually you can start over with another box.

Keeping Up With Letha

You are invited to take advantage of my work. I sift through scientific information, simplify it, make it useful, and then share it to benefit children, families, teachers; and all those who work with and care about children, their development, and their wellbeing.

Join in this process by:

• Liking my Facebook page https://www.facebook.com/Letha-Marchetti and staying in touch.

• You can find out more about me, my books, and my other publications, as well as contact me regarding speaking engagements and consultation through my treatment website: www.OccupationalTherapy-Letha.com

• Study with me at www.LethaMarchetti.com
Start with a free training and see what else is offered to propel your success to new levels.

• Let me know how this book helped you and what more you need.

• You have my gratitude for what you have done and are doing for our children.

Thanks for reading this. Please post a review on Amazon!

Great Resources!

• *The Out-of-Sync Child Has Fun* by Carol Stock Kranowitz

One of the most helpful and consistently useful books I have found for both early childhood educators and parents learning to support developing children.

This book gives an overview of seven senses. It offers checklists to clarify what the child is experiencing and relates the sensory experience to the child's behavior. The bulk of the book is fun activities keyed to sensory benefits.

• *Dragons & Daisies: Preschool Fun and Games*
   by Letha Marchetti OTR/L

Activities designed to work with developing nervous systems to find and maintain self-control. With sections for Easily Overwhelmed Children, Group Activities, even Nap-Time Help, this is a must have reference for everyone who works with young children.

• www.kidsinthehouse.com

Online help, free of charge, in short (often less than two minutes) video segments from experts. This site provides thousands of useful parenting videos and there's something for everyone who cares about children.

• *Trauma Through a Child's Eyes*
   by Peter A. Levine PhD and Maggie Kline

This thorough book provides understanding of the concept of experiencing our sensations so we can be whole. It offers activities for children to work through their experiences while gaining strength and confidence.

• *The Body Keeps the Score:*
Brain, Mind and Body in the Healing of Trauma
by Bessel Van Der Kolk, MD

If the child you are concerned about has been through a profound overwhelming experience and you need serious resources pick up this book. It is an engaging read that will increase your compassion for and understanding of those who have been traumatized.

Notes of Gratitude

For the numerous people who supported bringing this book to your hands, I am grateful.

Angela Ballard, thank you for your binge editing; for putting your life aside to tend to this project, and encouraging me in the process. Your skill and polish were vital.

Madeleine Schwab, you have encouraged, constructively criticized and helped clarify my work. You declared our serendipitous meeting in an airporter bus "bashert," (divinely destined). You were correct.

Martha and Warren Dayton, your skill and humor have brought life to Aiden and D. Dragon. I deeply appreciate the expertise with which you support me and this project.

William Nelken; thank you "Mr. Word Crafter" for your fresh set of eyes and willingness to apply your skills to this manuscript. You have made it clearer and better.

Colleen Ostergren, for showing me a new road, walking it with me and making it possible for this work to become something eminently tangible; I extend to you my gratitude.

Richard Marchetti, thank you for bearing up during the many phases of this project, especially those that required long hours with a computer. I love you fervently.

The Living God, for opening my eyes to what has been staring me in the face for decades. Jesus set the tone for my life by loving me just as I am and supporting me to develop, just as we do with children when we teach with love. The Bible tells us there is a time for each thing. I am excited that the time for this has come.

CPSIA information can be obtained
at www.ICGtesting.com
Printed in the USA
LVOW05*0057091216
516179LV00004B/4/P